Impossible
To
Forget

Julie Pujol-Karel

Lulu Press, Inc.

Printed by Lulu Press, Inc.
Library of Congress Cataloging-in-Publication Data
Pujol-Karel, Julie I.
Imposible Olvidar/Impossible to Forget
Library of Congress Catalog Card Number
Txu1-116-769
Printed in the United States of America
ISBN: 978-0-6151-6181-5

Impossible to Forget

Poems Collection

Dedicated To Romance –
To God -
Family and Friends –
And Diverse Themes-

Through out all generations,
Every human being, children, and adults alike,
Are in need of feeling the greatest gift of all,
That gift is LOVE.

Each page of this book brings a message, LOVE.

For you dear readers with LOVE.

Julie Ann I. Pujol-Karel

A few words from The Writer

This book is my dream converted to reality, but would not have been possible if it is not for the moral and spiritual support received from my family and friends.

This is dedicated to my parent's memory Mr. Jose E. Pujol and Mrs. Antonia M. Del Campo. My father wrote poetry as well, but was not able to publish his poetry.

To the memory of my husband, Jan Karel M.D., he was the reason for my English poems, because he was not able to understand my writings in my native tongue.

To my son and daughter Nestor R. and Janett J. especially Janett, She is the editor of the English section of the book. To My son – in - law Gary and my daughter – in - law Darci. To my five grandchildren, Julianna, Alan, Nicholas, Joshua and Aracely; with the desire to be known by them not just as "grandmother", but as a poet with feelings, thoughts, beliefs and convictions.

To my five sisters Célida, Elia, Aleida, Gladys and Oilda who patiently have listened to me and my poetry, while this book was in the making countless times. To all my nephews and nieces that equally have given me the courage to complete the book by telling me "yes you can".

To my friends, too many to be named, they equally had encouraged me and listened to my poetry for years. My special thanks goes to Cheryl Byrne, she has helped me unconditionally to see my dream come true. Josie Elks, Anne Siefken, Lupe & Pepe Sangerman, Diane Pieranunzi, they believed in this project, and me.

I would like to express my most sincere gratitude to Ms. Celita Gómez, the woman that kept a small group of Cubans in unity through her gatherings at "Café De La Habana". She brought us together to celebrate special occasions, to read poetry, to joke, and to converse.

Above all, my gratefulness goes to God. "Everything is possible through God that strengthens me" Philippians 4:13. Without him, this book would not be in your hands today.

To my readers with love

Julie Pujol-Karel

TABLE OF CONTENTS

Romantic Poems

DIVERSE THEMES

Romantic
Poems

Always You

The trees were lacking their beautiful green foliage –
The naked branches were crying for
a bit of sunshine.

Just like the trees were crying,
begging for the rebirth of their foliage –
My soul filled with melancholy
was also crying for what was left behind.

Below, the streets were becoming
smaller and smaller through my tears.
Prague, the beautiful old city –
disappeared at last, out of sight.

More over, when I closed my eyes,
I discovered -
That not every thing
was left behind.

No, forevermore I brought with me…
Deeply seeded in the pupil of my eyes,
dressed in a beige gabardine,
and a pair of blue jeans
the figure of my man-

Tonight

My anxious body moves beneath the blanket.
The light I have turned off, but I cannot sleep.
I have extended an arm to turn on the small lamp,
Immediately, my eyes move to locate him.

Yes, he is there –
His picture hangs on the white wall.
I cannot avoid it.
I get up slowly to touch him.

My lips are kissing now the cold glass –
And when I kiss his nose, eyes and forehead,
A warm heat takes over my body.

I returned to bed quietly –
Bringing with me his image embedded in my retinas.
My heart tells me –
"You will always love him as much as you did".

Now What

Now that you flew over oceans,
and mountain peaks –
Now that so many miles,
separates your body from mine.

Tell me…can you sleep in peace at night?
After all the pain and sorrows
You brought to my life.

Is there anything left inside of you…
That might remind you now of me?
In a kind or sweet manner
as it should be.

Have you found my pictures in an old scrapbook
Or a forgotten card with a poem written,
for you by me?

Have you found the courage to admit?
You could have been happy at last…
But you blew it all away.
Well…I guess it does not matter any more.

Birds Fly Free

Birds fly free but they have a nest –

Every day to their nest, they return.

What a wonderful feeling,
to be free in the spirit.
But to share and care each day
with some one, that loves you the same.

The Lord has made us for each other –
To share and care with everlasting love,
one for another.

Feeling

I know I am feeling blue –
But really, I am feeling you.
So come on,
I know you are feeling blue…
About me, too.
Come on I know it's true.

*Note-My granddaughter Julianna Baxter wrote this poem.
At age nine.

Hate I Cannot

I wish to hate him,
but hate I cannot –
Impossible is to hate,
the man you love.

Painful is to see him,
distant and cold,
I need his embrace…
I need his love.

My life has become,
a true dilemma.
Could I live again if I let him go?

Can I break the chains that hold me steadfast?
My mind tells me **YES,**
My heart tells me **IMPOSSIBLE.**

I Can't Forget

I can't forget...
Your memories haunt me,
I can't forget
the way we meet
so long ago sweet heart.

And I can't forget...
The way your eyes shinned so bright,
your smiling face and then,
the way you tried to trick me into "bed"

I can't forget...
The way you asked me again and again.
Sweet heart –
It was hard to resist your charm.
But I could not consent so suddenly.
Nevertheless, **I CAN'T FORGET**.

I Never Will

Don't ever think...
That I'll return some day,
Don't ever dream of it,
'Cause I never will.

Don't ever say...
That I have spoken badly about you...
You well deserved it –
But I never had and I never will.

Sadly enough,
It is what you have said and done regarding me.
Nevertheless –
Don't think that I have not forgiven you...
Of course I did.

You see-
I need to pray each night,
To my God above,
He would not listen if I don't **FORGIVE.**
But don't ever ask me to return to the nest,
I never will.

I Will Not Say A Word

I will depart one day,
when my heart no longer can take your apathy-
As the sun disappears,
behind the mountains, behind the sea.

Without saying a word…
some day I will depart from thee.
You will not find me with every sunrise,
I will not return when the sun goes down.

Every woman has a great need –
Deeply seeded within her soul,
it has nothing to do
with jewels, silver or gold.
She needs to feel the warmth of his love,
The love of the man –
She chose long ago.

**These verses are for you –
Dedicated to your memory.**

With these words, I wish to express…
A love story, our own story.

You had gone away to meet with your maker.
He will give you the peace you were searching for.

My love cannot reach you now –
Not my pain or my tears.
But you are enjoying the peace that you needed my
dear.

I have loved you forever-
My love for you remains.
One day our eyes will meet,
In heaven again.

In My Dreams

Last night as I lay on my empty bed –
To the Lord I prayed,
that you will visit my dreams…
To fill them with your magic,
and love that is divine.

The time passed by slowly –
I could not fall asleep.
While my wandering mind
remembered your kisses.

As dawn drew near,
weariness took over me –
My eyelids were feeling heavy,
closing my eyes finally.

Just as the breeze,
without even noticing
I had fallen asleep.

You came to my dreams –
Just as I had prayed,
Your warm breath I felt so close to me!
I awakened suddenly…
Thinking my love,
that you were with me.

Jealousy

I wrote of our love on the sand of a beach.
The waves got jealous
And washed the words away.

I wrote of our love on a mountain peak,
It was filled with snow.
The sun became so jealous,
And melted the snow away.

I wrote of our love on the leaves of a tree,
The winds of autumn came,
Leaving the tree bare.

I got angry at the waves of the sea,
At the melting snow and the autumn leaves.

Then, I wrote your love in my heart –
I hid it so well, never to be found…
Except by the person to which this love belongs.

Look For Me #1

Look for me behind your shadow,
Within the retina of your clear eyes.
Look for me between your fingers,
Or over your Sandalwood lips.

I am like a breath of life-
Seeded deeply within you.
It is useless to deny you love me too.

Look for me in your bedroom
Even if another woman
Is using the pillow that used to be mine.

Look for me in your dreams:
When you have no control of your actions and
thoughts.
Or by the road you are walking along –
Although another woman, might be walking beside
you.

LOOK FOR ME.

Look For Me Again #2

Yes my Love **"Look for Me"**
Because even ignoring these feelings,
That your pride attempts to suffocate –
You will find me,
I never went away.

I will be in your mind,
By the blue flowers you might find at springtime,
By the meadows or prairies as you are walking by.

You will find me again and again –
While looking at the moon and to the stars.
I am within your soul,
You have sealed our love in your heart,
It cannot be denied.
It is useless and in vain to try.

Look for Me #3

That you could not find me in winter or spring.
! Oh! Wait until summer time –
You will find me indeed.

As you are sailing different waters,
Away from me –
You will remember with melancholy,
The many summers we have shared together
In each other's company.

Your brown eyed girl,
Waited ashore, by the salty waters of the blue sea.
Or under the shadows of our favorite tree-

That you cannot find me.
Try again...
And <u>stop</u> kidding yourself.
Look For Me.
I live in your memories.

Memories

I am too far from the ocean, and the waves of the
blue sea.
From the white and soft sand
Where long ago, I had buried my feet.

I am so far, so far away
From the bay and the old green tree,
The tree that gave us shade each summer
While we both rested and kissed.

Sometimes you went wind surfing,
I tagged along with you,
The salty waters caressed our bodies and also the
wind.
Many other instances I stayed ashore to see you
surfing with the wind.

Those summer days are over with,
Yet so alive inside of me
That if I only close my eyes,
With certainty, I can feel…
My wet feet buried in the sand,
The wind caressing me
And I can also feel your kisses salty, soft, and warm
over my lips.

Misfit To Love

You were so great in many ways...
But sadly, enough now I can say,
You did not love yourself
What else could I expect?
You were **misfit to love.**

Years passed and I stayed,
With the hope to find your inner depth.
The door to your soul
I found closed each time,
It hurt me so much that I ran away.

My love for you was never enough,
A love so profound that no one understood.
Always returned empty,
Because your love lacked,

Abundant were your gifts,
In that I never lacked –
I did not want gifts,
Only the kisses you never gave.

Perhaps it was not your fault.
How can you give what you never had?
You were empty of feelings –
Misfit to love.

Missing You

I will miss your eyes,
I will miss your smile,
I will miss your embrace,
Each day each night
Spring, summer, fall, and winter.

I will miss your look,
I will miss your gaze,
That undressed me invisibly.

I will miss your smile, warm and tender,
Spoke of a desire always burning within you.

I will miss your embrace, soft and strong,
At the same time.

No words could express,
What it meant to me each day each night.

I will miss you completely –
The way we loved each other,
The way we both made love.
But memories don't die.
So you will be with me although you are gone.

On Track

I picked up where we had left before –
His warm body wrapped in mine,
In silence, I heard his voice…
He told me things he never said before.

The closeness of his body,
Has aroused in me –
Feelings and sensations,
Dormant within me.

And it started again,
Where we had left.
Patience and acceptance
It is always the best.

Our Mutual Feelings

I was so busy with my pain,
Feeling self pity for myself,
I was so sad that my dreams were crumbling –
And I did not realize that you also felt hurt.

Because a nest is built by two –
And some how I felt that I did not count,
I did not realize that your dreams as well
Were crumbling down as much as mine were –
And yes, you had invited me to participate,
I just could not see it then.

How foolish can we be at times?
We hear but we don't listen –
You also were crying inside,
But I did not see it or hear it.

Last night I finally listened to you…
I feel that now we are even,
I can really give it a chance,
Both of us shared the same feelings.
Now I can see that our love –
Was mutual from the beginning.

Poem of the Years

When years pass by,
And you remember me only
Sleep deep in memories of yesterday.
Close your green-gray eyes slowly,
And think of all those years
That we enjoyed together,
And will never return.

Perhaps at that instant
You'll ask to yourself the question,
Why didn't I make the effort
To keep this love alive?

When the years pass by
And somehow, for some reason,
You remember that I was a part of your yesterday.
Close serene and tranquil your beautiful green-gray
eyes,
And think of all those years,
That never will return.

Prisoner of Love

Prisoner of Love I live.
Although I am free to come and go,
As I so choose and desire –
I am a prisoner of Love.

He is with me.
Wherever I go,
I cannot take his body-
But I take him in my soul.

Prisoner I feel,
And I cannot help it.
Prisoner of a love that is consuming me.
I wish I could, but I cannot shake it.

Long ago he told me,
"That He Loves Me So"
But never again I have felt the warmth of his touch.

How I wish to forget him,
But forget I cannot.
For that reason I live **PRISONER OF LOVE.**

The Hat

No, no one sits on the couch...
The hat lay on a cushion already dusty.

Somewhere in the quiet room –
The knees are bending,
The cheeks are wet, but the chin is high
The eyes are lifted to the sky.

The voice as a murmur,
Continues to plead…
To the God Almighty
To whom she speaks.

Many months have gone by,
And in the same quiet room –
The hat lay on the couch on the same cushion.

The name of a man is heard many times,
And the voice is praising **"The Almighty God"**.
The man she loves is on the way to recovery.
It is best to know that he is doing well -
Although, perhaps forever far away from her.

What Did You Think?

What did you think?
Perhaps that my love for you,
Will last forever?

If you don't water a garden,
The flowers die,
The wind will blow the flowers away-
Dust will remain.

You mistreated our love-
You forgot to nourish it,
With caresses and kisses…
We never made love again.

What did you expect?
That it would last forever?
No, it could not be so,
Now only dust remains –

For lack of attention,
My love for you is **GONE.**

When Death Brings Us Apart

When death brings us apart,
to you and her,
to him and me...
Could we begin again and reunite?
No one but **God Himself**
can answer that question.

When death brings us apart,
to you and her,
to him and me
I have no idea how long I will wait for that –

Or who will go first, second or third...?
I only know, that when the fourth one
Is gone at last...
We will reunite again in the stars.

So...I live at peace...with no regrets.
I did what I had to do yesterday.
But I am looking forward to the future,
to the City of Pearls and Emerald Seas –
There I will be reunited again with you.

When Years Go By

When years go by,
And you feel lonely and empty,
It would be perhaps at that moment
That you will remember me –

Then you should compare,
If someone has ever loved you, before or after,
As much as I did.

The answer will knock at your conscience –
Bitter, painful and clear.
No, no one has ever loved me
As much as she did.

When years go by –
And your youth is gone,
And your honey-brown hair
Changes to silver strings.

Close your eyes for a moment
Remember my brown eyes,
Your inner voice will ask you –
Why did I let her go?
Perhaps she was not perfect,
But did love me so.

Why? #1

Why do I have to love him?
He never did –
Why do I miss him so?
He never had.
Why do I suffer?
He does not care.

Why do I dream of him?
It is not fair.
Why do I have to remember him?
Day, night, awake, or in my sleep?
He never did and never will –

Why did I find such a man?
I should not love him –
But I love him still.
Why?

Why Lord? #2

Why do I love him Lord?
He is so indifferent-
Why do I love him still?
He is acting so cold.

The bed that we once shared,
It seems that we take turns to use it.
He has always excuses –
And explains to me why not.

"It is nothing against you my dear"
He tells me every morning.
You know I was too busy,
And had fallen asleep on my chair.
"It is nothing against you my dear"
I can swear it.

And I have waited for him, each night, useless
dream.
Although I know within my heart -
He is not coming back.

You Are My Inspiration

I gave my life to you long ago.
Today again I pledge my life to you…
Forever and always,
I am flesh of your flesh.

The storms of life have blown strong,
But I will stand to the test.
I am bone of your bones,
Flesh of your flesh.

Cause I stand on "Holy Ground"
Whatever comes our way…
I will wait for you so patiently,
I don't need to search –
For someone else.

The Lord has given me to you –
And you to me,
For richer or for poorer,
In health and in sickness,
To share and to hold.

Today again, I pledge my love to you –
Forever and always,
Sweet Love.

You Need To Spread Your Wings

You need to spread your wings like an eagle.
You need to be again the man you used to be.
Somehow along the path,
You have lost your way-
And laid the burden of responsibilities,
To be carried out by someone else.

Although my love for you,
Will remain forever within my soul-
I have no other choice but to let you go.
In order for you to regain the place,
That you should have,
And somehow you have lost.
"You need to spread your wings my love"

You

You were too precious and too kind,
A man of great compassion –
Perhaps not always understood by others…
But I knew you well and realized,
That you belonged with the Angels above.

You have left us in pain,
And I will miss you forever –
But I know it was best for you…
Your suffering is over.

Now you are embraced
In the wings of love.
Who knew your heart best? -
The Lord your maker **MY LOVE.**

No one could match what I felt for you,
No one understood why either.
But you gave always your all –
For those who have none,
It has given you the place,
You have won in my heart,
FOREVER.

You'll Never Know

You'll never know
That I love you still,
You don't deserve it,
But I see you in my dreams.

You'll never know
That I love you still,
Across the miles, the oceans,
And across the wind.

I cannot forget you
Although I have tried,
My intents were useless,
You are in my mind.

But you will never know
That I love you so –
Because you don't deserve it.
That much I know.

Themes
Diverse

Angels On Earth

On a Halloween day an Angel was born –
Crowned with an invisible Halo,
Transparent wings.

She brought light to the house
Of the humble parents,
They received the task of raising an Angel.

The Cherub grew up
In the shape of a woman…
Her Halo and Her Wings
Were transparent.

It could only be seen,
By those who know her well –
By those that she cares for; those that she helps.

Her earthly name is: "Cheryl"
She is my friend…
This Angel was born on a Halloween Day.

Note: Dedicated to my friend Cheryl with sincere appreciation and love for all the things she has done for me unselfishly.

I Am Back Again

I never thought I 'd be back again –
To the place where I began my life in the USA.
I never thought I 'd see this Land again
Or hear the thunders roar.

Here I am –
I did not plan it this way.
But I am so glad to see these plains,
The greenery of its grasses.
To see and feel the falling rain,
The land, where I began to live again.

I Don't Know

How did I start to write poems?
I don't know.
I only know that I was on a flight –
Destination, a new way of life,
My old life left behind.

Not too many miles I was crossing,
But I knew that at the end of the flight
A new life was waiting for me.
A new language I would hear…
I became afraid.

Many different things I would find –
I would have to get accustomed to all that.
It was the first time that I was alone,
Away from my family and friends,
Leaving all the things I knew behind.

It was on that occasion that…
I found myself writing a poem.
It was during that short trip,
That later on changed my life forever –
I was asking to the **Universal God,**
Not to leave me alone, **NEVER.**

The Military Days

To My Daughter

The days you were serving in the Military
"Desert Storm"
I'll never forget.
I spent whole nights on prayers
Asking the Lord to bring you home safe.

The experiences you have lived,
Have made you very strong –
You have grown-up so fast
My daughter, my love.

I am so proud of you,
So proud that you are my own –
My precious little girl,
Now a woman self sufficient on her own.

The White Rose

Today I went to the garden
To see, if the roses had bloomed…
I wanted to cut a few for her.

The weather left a lot to be desired–
The falling rain soon soaked my clothes,
That stuck to my body as gloves stick to fingers.
I felt trembling to the bones.

A warm vapor was escaping from the earth through
the wet grass.
I stood there for a long time, static, enjoying the
elements,
Rain, wind, thunder, and lightening.

The roses had bloomed.
Every color imaginable was on display,
Peach, strawberry red and pink,
The yellow rose of Texas as well.

But my greatest joy was to see
"The White rose" in clusters.
I had purchased the particular rose bush
To honor her memory.

When I saw the "White rose" -
It was as if she was there
so pure, so beautiful.

I felt the warm vapor exhaling from the earth,
Through the wet grass, I felt the warmth of her
embrace -
While the rain drops where bathing my body,
It felt like being bathed in her presence by her love.

Oh! The Beautiful "White rose"-
Unique among all others…
It brought remembrances to my mind.

Carefully, I had chosen the roses to be cut;
Placing them later on, in a transparent crystal vase.
Transparent as her soul was.

I then placed the vase in front of her picture-
My favorite one…
It appears as if she was walking away from the
frame,
laughing amusingly, talking again.

What a beautiful time I have passed in the garden!
Feeling her presence through the elements;
Rain, wind, thunder, and lightening.

Pretending to hear her voice softly scolding me,
"don't get wet"
I don't wish for you to get sick.

The years have continued to pass since she passed
away.
Yes I know that she is gone
I was only pretending that she was there with me….
After all forever present she will be,
In my heart, within my soul and "In the Garden".

Poem of a Sad Land

Castro: Evildoer,
You have betrayed your people.
When you returned from your hideaway in the mountains,
A Christian Cross was hanging from your neck.

Again it is July 26th, -"**Revolution Day**" you celebrate.
By force, the workers are removed from their work place.
Forced to ride on trucks, to the "The Public Square"-
Behind their backs, sharp machete points too close to their bodies -
Who dares to complain?

Years pass by, you put on the same show,
So the world can conclude that
The Cubans on the island are in agreement with
Whatever you do, say, or think until today.

Castro, evildoer –
You are lying to yourself.
Hidden is the reality due to hardness of spirit,
Self centered **egocentric beast.**

How dare you say, **"The revolution had triumphed"?**
In Cuba the children walk barefoot.
Bread lacks in every home.
No clothes are hung in the wardrobes.

The tractors have disappeared.
Plowing the land manually has returned.
Mal-nourished men push the plow,
The bulls are badly fed as well.

Arrogant are your speeches…
"The medical field has progressed"
It is all a fairy tale, "the sad reality I must tell"
Unexpectedly, physicians must perform surgeries,
Aided by an oil lamp, the electricity goes off often.
Doctors lack the anesthesia needed many times.

The Cubans cannot depend on,
Even to watch a television show.
When they are least expecting it,
The electricity turns off.
Castro: evildoer

Shells

I hear the sound of the ocean –
Listen sh sh sh – can you hear it?
Ah, the cool breeze is caressing my body.
I am wet, happy, playing **with shells.**

Can you see it?
All colors, sizes, and shapes.
Do you see the tiny spirals?
Oh, some are broken, but others are intact.

Beautiful creatures of the sea,
have lived inside these crusts
now empty lifeless,
scattered over sand.

The ocean pushes them beyond their native realm
with the waves.
But then, the same waves gather them back,
sweeping it again, and again.
Why? They are empty vessels now, lifeless.

Empty shells once filled with life and energy.
Now delight in children's little hands –
And adults such as I who walk miles

without realizing how far I went,
in search of the **"Perfect Shell"**.

Tomorrow, perhaps a few of these pieces will be
carefully drilled in the center,
inserted with a strong thread, converted into
necklaces.
The work will be done no doubt by the hands of
Hong Kong women, Philippines, Indonesian,
Guatemalan, and Mexicans –
Who knows?

Then, shells on display on American young ladies'
necks.
As for myself, I am keeping one close to me,
So I can hear the sound of the ocean through my
favorite "Shell"
Sh sh sh – can you hear the sound?
I brought the ocean with me **in a shell.**

In Solidarity

Women are like the gamma of the spectrum –
All colors, different shapes and sizes,
But the heart and soul are all alike
When they come together to unify.

Life is a rainbow and a collage –
The birds, the flowers, the butterflies.
They are all so different, and yet so beautiful.
They live together in harmony.

We are together with one idea –
We can make changes within our union,
To make it better in the near future
For all our members not for a few.

Have faith in yourself and in **"Our Father"**
We can make a difference in the life of others
If we continue to work
"In Solidarity"

Wedding Day

Archangels were singing a song of joy –
The sound of a harp was softly heard –
From the violins the sweet notes came…
And voices were saying, **"The Lord has heard"**

Yes, he has listened to Lynn's prayers.
And she has prayed for so long –
To send her a man that is honest and true.
Strong in the **Word**, Strong in the **Lord.**

Bells are ringing for Lynn at last –
With faith in **God** she has chosen right.
This is a wedding made up in **Heaven.**
Blessed by **God** it will last forever.

Separation

It is time dear Mother
The trumpet has sounded for your redemption.
The Eternal God full of mercy,
Has sent Angels to free your spirit.

No longer will you feel pain,
Now you rest tranquil –
Gold streets your feet are walking.

Today you have joined the rest of the family,
Those loved ones that have departed.
Long before yesterday.

I will miss you –
Dear Mother.
I will miss you as long as I live;
But I feel tranquil,
I have the assurance that one day in the future…
Again we will meet.

It is worth it to accept Jesus,
And his salvation gift.
Our bodies will wither,
But our souls will be renewed –
Eternal Life we have in the Lord.

I See Them

I see them
Their sad faces I have seen through the window,
While I was traveling in a train;
Yes I have seen them…
Soiled clothes, hair unkempt.
A bitter smile adorning their faces.

I see them
Each day every where –
On every corner, along the alleyway.
Searching in trashcans for food, for cigarettes.

I see them
Sitting at the curb of a sidewalk, or under a tree –
Perhaps too tired to walk any longer,
Trying to rest.

As I look at them with each passing day –
I think that these people weary, tired, not properly
feed
They are also my brothers,
Citizens of this Country as well.

Celebration

How wonderful it is to celebrate –
The Birth of **Jesus,**
When he came to this world
He brought us peace and love.
He brought hope to a lost world.
Forgiveness of sins and salvation he brought.

I am very thankful to **Jesus.**
He extends me his hands with every sunrise.
He tells me **"don't be afraid"**
I am with you-
And as certain as I was born,
One day I will return.

Don't Give Up

Don't give up – Don't quit,
Keep on striving – Keep up your faith.

The trophy I hold in my hands today,
It is the result of:
Years of writing and striving –
Years of praying to the "almighty" –
Not losing my vision,
Not losing my faith.

Oh don't give up – Don't quit,
There are rainbows ahead of you to be reached.

You are never too young – Never too old,
Age is only a state of the mind.
God sees all of us as a child.

Don't give up – Don't quit,
Be all that you dreamed to be.
It is "God's Will" –
For you to reach your dreams.

Conversing With God

Lord you never told me that life was easy –
Or you never told me that life was free of pain,
But I remember when one day you told me
"I will give you strength every step of the way".

My heart was rejoicing with my husband's
homecoming –
Every morning I felt like a new bride…
But this afternoon the devil passed by,
Attempted to disturb me, he has no right.

I learned that my father is sick –
He feels so lonesome because he misses mom,
I can share his feelings…
I am also missing my dear mom.

But I do thank you Lord –
Don't misunderstand,
I am forever grateful that she went home with you.
I know how much she loved you,
And also knew of her suffering,
My strength comes from the fact
That she is resting with you.

There is other news I like to share with you.
My nephew left the country,
Drifting on the ocean, his vessel is a raft –
He is looking for freedom of speech and religion
Oh Lord bring me good news that he is safe, alive,
Under your everlasting care and protective eyes.

It seems so Far Away

It seems so far away…
Yet everyone could benefit from His teachings.
It seems so far away…
Yet it could be a better world,
If we abide by His preaching.

It seems so far away …
Nevertheless His preaching
Applies to every life today.
It will be a better world today if we listen –

He has spoken of peace,
He has spoken of love –
He spoke of giving more than receiving.

Get along with your family,
And with your neighbors –
If we all do the same,
No Wars but Peace will result.

Give love to your family,
Give love to your neighbors
Hatred will end and you will be a better person.

Give all that you can –
Love, Time, Effort…
If we all do the same it will be a better world.
Filled with Love and Contentment, no Resentment.

My Lord

How do I love you oh Lord all Mighty –
How do I love you my Lord,
For being so patient.
How do I love you Lord for your forgiveness…
You do cleanse my sins with every dawn.
You cleanse my soul when the sun goes down.

How do I love you Lord –
For the eternal life that so undeserving you have
offered…
To every one accepting your sacrifice.

How painful it must have been –
TO BE NAILED ON A CROSS.
How great is your love.
Moreover, as your life was expiring on that cross,
You were cleansing our SINS my sweet LORD.

Merry Christmas

"Merry Christmas"
A man told me,
Dressed-up in a fine gabardine and a new hat.

"Merry Christmas"
A woman passing by told me, she had a great smile.
You could tell that the shoes she was wearing were a
good brand.
An expensive fur covered her shoulders this winter
night.

"Merry Christmas"
A young man told me,
His clothes were old and soiled, filled with grime.

"Merry Christmas"
Smiling a poor woman told me
Her body poorly covered with rags.
She was walking barefoot in the cold starry night.

"Merry Christmas" I answered –
Yes, Merry Christmas every one…
Because I know deep in my soul,
That one-day no too far…
Those barefoot and in rags –
They will be dressed-up too,
Shinning like the stars.

Big Bear Lake

Pine crested earth – they're so high above, hidden
away from the naked eye,
A narrow winding road- Only one-way to arrive, the
same to return.

Small log houses dot the woods.
Devised, from time to time, if their lights were on.

Pine trees – so tall! Your neck must arch back if you
want to see
The fullness of their majesty.

The crusted earth reflects shimmering white –
The moon is full, constellations shine in the dark sky.
I want to take it all in! I want to remember this sight
as long as I live.

Cold starry night, so peaceful, I'm close to heaven yet
millions of miles away.
After much reflection I enter the pub, sawdust covers
the wooden floor.
It's warm inside - three chimneys at work in full
force.

Thick logs are burning, red blazes making figurines, dancing tongues.
Wood sparkles, crackling noise, smell of hickory.

Taking my gloves off, I ask the bartender for an Irish Cream coffee.
I sat on the stool so high that my feet dangle.
I finished my Irish Cream coffee, encased my hands in my old gloves.
I needed to go, but not before taking a closer look at the place;
The sturdy wooden seats, the shimmering chimney,
Sawdust covers the wooden floor.

The music is loud – a few people are dancing,
Their boots breaking the peace, the tranquility of my surroundings.
Boots – the people are dancing in their boots.

I finally went out and stared at the sky.
Full moon, startling night, the stars filling the sky.
The snow gleaming now covering completely the pine-crusted earth.
I wanted to take it all in, breathing the cold area I continue on my journey
Until I can find "Big Bear Lake".

Nothing but Blessings

What a blessing it is to be
Resurrected with the Lord –
I feel renewed,
The storms have passed away,
Leaving memories of sweet and bitter days,
It formed part of my life,
It cannot be erased.

Beautiful it is to see
A clear road ahead –
Where the sun shines for you,
And does not hurt.

When you lift your eyes to see around you,
And you can visualize…
The woods, the splendor plains of green,
I can feel the reality of **GOD** –
It is then that I can see with clarity,
And know he made it all for you and me.

Returned to the Lord

I was so busy with things not everlasting
I had run from place to place, with feeling of
emptiness.
Had lost my way some how –
I could not find the path, to happiness.

Every night I felt so empty,
I cried myself to sleep,
Every morning I had awakened –
With the hope to find the joy I had lost.
A joy that surpasses human understanding,
It had been mine so long ago.

I prayed but did not get an answer –
At least I could hear not one.
Sometimes I cried in agony,
I needed the presence of the Lord in me.

Where did I go wrong Heavenly Father?
How have I lost my way?
It is not the story of Hansel and Gretel
They spread breadcrumbs to find their way again.

Then I heard his voice…
Sweeter than ever, I could say –
Herein is what He said.
I have never left you,
My love does not change,
Forever I love you, I am the same.

Oh! I have returned to my maker,
I have returned to my Lord –
My life is no longer empty.
The Holy Spirit has filled me with joy.

Your Are My Light

You are my light –
You are the reason why I breathe each day.
You are my song, the birds sing to your majesty.
I follow suit and praise your name.

You are my guide –
You are the reason, the hand that changes the
seasons,
And you have changed my life.

Springtime comes, and from the earth pastures
unroll –
A soft green carpet of grass
On which children play, cattle graze.
Flowers perfume the ambience wherever you walk;
Butterflies wings moving from flower to flower with
the soft wind.

And pretty soon beaches are filled,
Laughter and music, nets and balls,
With buckets and pails children play,
Majestic sandcastles are seen ashore.

The aroma of the barbecues impregnate the air –
Hamburgers, hotdogs, the grills are filled with
roasted corn.
It is summer time for every soul –
For the old, the young, the rich, and the poor.

Now, it is time to reflect, to think, to rest a bit –
The leaves are falling from the Maple trees covering
the ground,
The Golden color of the autumn leaves reminds me
That winter time and holidays are near.

Oh! winter days you do bring the snow –
Tiny flakes sparkling with the sun.
No one can make it except the Lord.
Winter and the holidays are here,
And I will celebrate with ecstasy and joy,
The birth of my King, of Jesus My Lord.

Recognitions

Poets Northwest - 19th Annual Spring Fling 2006 – Poems for Old Lovers.

First Place for "Look for Me".

Third Place for "Memories".

Poetry Society of Texas – Houston Chapter - Winter Poetry Festival – 2005

The HAP Fulgham Award - First Place for "Shells".

Lucidity Poetry Journal Award –Second Place for "Mourning".

Southwest Writers Club – (Writing Competition) – 2005

First Place for "The White Rose"- "La Rosa Blanca".

Third Place for "Castro"- "Poem of a Sad Land".

Houston Poetry Fest – 2004

University of Houston/Houston Art Endowment.

Juried Poet – for "Exilio" "Exile".

Southwest Writers Club - (Writing Competition) – 2004

First Place for "Memories".

Second Place for "You are My Light".

<u>Southwest Writers Club</u> - (Writing Competition) – 2003

First Place for "A Hearth Filled with Joy".

<u>International Library of Poets</u> – 2003

Editor's Choice – First Place – For "As Years Go By".

<u>International Library of Poets</u> – 2002

Editor's Choice – First Place for "Don't Give-Up".

Publications in Anthologies

2006 – The Long and the Short of It – Poets Northwest.
    Poems - "Rodin" y "A Guiding Light"

2006 – Windows - University of Houston – Alvin Campus.
    Poem – "Big Bear Lake".

2006 – Laberinto de Sentimientos -Centro Poético – Madrid,
España
    Poem – "Esta Noche".

2006 – Miradas de Nostalgia - Centro Poético – Madrid,
España
    Poem - Amor de Siempre.

2005 – Tracing the Infinite - International Library of Poetry.
    Poem – "Prisoner of Love".

2005 – Aurora – Centro Poético – Madrid, España
    Poem – "Cruz Liviana".

2005 – The Arts Alliance Center – Clear Lake, Texas
    "Exhibition by the Square Foot"
    Poems Exhibited -"Shells", "Memories" and "You Are
    My Light"
    "Art by the Square Foot" Chap Book.

2005 – Houston Poetry Fest – Outbound Series – Webster,
Texas

Juried Poet – Poems – Fate, Danube River, Opposite Poles, A Child at the Astro's Dome, New Orleans Tragedy.

2004 - Houston Poetry Fest (Nineteenth Anniversary)
    Juried Poet - Poem – "Exilio" "Exile".

2004 – On the Wings of Poetry – Famous Poets (Lavander-Aurora)
    Poem "When Years Go By".

2004- Poems of the World – Palatine, Illinois
    Poem – "Returned to the Lord" autumn

2004- Poems of the World – Palatine, Illinois
    Poem – "Look for Me #2" spring

2003 - Poems of the World – Palatine, Illinois
    Poem - "Look for Me #1

2003 – The Color of Life - International Library of Poetry.
    Poem – "Poem of the Years".

Member of The Poetry Society of Texas – Houston Chapter and Northwest Chapter.

Invited often by "Nuestra Palabra" radio program sponsored by The Arts and Literacy of Houston, station KPFT, Tuesday 7:00 PM, and also by the local radio station 920AM program "Entérate" from 1:00 PM to 2:00 PM

Directs and participates in Poetry Jam for "The Hispanic Book Festival" – Annually, in February - Houston, TX.

Founder of "Conversing Through Poetry" poetry group that meets on the 2nd Wednesday of every month at 7:30 PM at Barnes & Noble Copperfield Store/Northwest Houston, Texas.

This book can be obtained At:

www.Amazon.com
Barnes & Noble
www.barnesandnoble.com
Borders
www.borders.com
www.Lulu.com

www.ingramcontent.com/pod-product-compliance
Lightning Source LLC
LaVergne TN
LVHW091208080426
835509LV00006B/884